T0381162

Life
Above
the
Few
Moments

TERRY CROWDER JR.

WESTBOW
PRESS®
A DIVISION OF THOMAS NELSON
& ZONDERVAN

WestBow Press books may be ordered through booksellers or by contacting:

WestBow Press
A Division of Thomas Nelson & Zondervan
1663 Liberty Drive
Bloomington, IN 47403
www.westbowpress.com
844-714-3454

ISBN: 979-8-3850-3124-5 (sc)
ISBN: 979-8-3850-3125-2 (e)

Library of Congress Control Number: 2024916649

Print information available on the last page.

WestBow Press rev. date: 10/15/2024

I dedicate this book to my grandmother, Christine Friday-Jones.
Secondly to the children of Djibouti who have
inspired me to keep smiling and growing.

CONTENTS

——— CHAPTER 1 ———
MOMENT OF THOUGHT

I remember the few moments that really meant something to me in life and what I learned from those valuable experiences. It's the few moments that make life worth the effort to live and to live it in a way that honors something greater than you. At the time, my "Greater "was my siblings, my mother and my dream that I would be able to change the lives of the ones I love for the better and truly forever. The few moments of decisions and choices come together like sand and heat; that ultimately give or provide you the clearer picture. There are a few moments of great passion, then there are moments of nothing. Those moments where I experienced solace, seems to breathe a tune of peace, placing me in a cloud of awareness of oneself that really in all honesty; only you and God know. You may not believe in God, but you do believe in feelings and emotions to steer your direction like a compass. That one direction will steer those precious few moments into something much bigger than yourself or make you think you are" bigger" than what you really are. The rich glorify being rich and the poor glorify the working class, but we only have a few moments to share. Regardless of your economic status, we are but a few moments. The few moments I have, I choose to glorify God fully in my being. He is Truth that gives you a task, a role, a connection, a home and a relationship uniquely all its own because of your persona designed by the Creator.

How do you describe the few moments that you value from your life? Please share your thoughts with me.

_____

_____

_____

_____

_____

The few moments that we have on this planet is special. The planet is unique in so many ways and it is perfectly woven into a valley that kisses the mountain that leaves you in awe of the craftsmanship. Technology has allowed us to see the planet in so many different angles and point of views; that help our minds grasp the complexity, intimacy, and precious few moments that we feel part of the world itself. It is perfection that inspire us to grow, chase, pursue and live with zeal that comes from acknowledging the perfect Creator. The one thing I have noticed, nothing that is man-made is eternal it must be maintained or updated to meet the conditions of the mindset of mankind to always move forward and to progress. People that choose to make the world better for the next generation, they desire something far greater than themselves. The irony of that statement is when you see death, violence and destruction that is endorsed by sin or wrongdoing, situations like that make it seem like that's the norm of human nature throughout history that describes the character of our ambition to change the world. Human perspective can only be positive or negative, separated by a fence of repetition and free will. Regardless of the independent variables that can affect our process of thinking about life situations, however we still have a choice to build, heal, or deprive and destroy for sake of perspective built on the foundation of knowledge, feelings, history and personal experiences. Who can say that their way of thinking or living in this world the perfect way to be. Only one man has stated the perfect way to live life and the mindset to have longevity. That longevity consists of disciplines, statutes, and instructions that are in tune with one true nature of Jesus Christ. Every law created in human history agrees with righteousness, peace and justice, in which they agree or align with bible verses instituted by the Lord. My studies of the Constitution, Bill of Rights, and the Emancipation Proclamation all align with the Word. I never understood where the origin of our laws came from. The influence or the catalyst of it, in which a person can dissect to see if laws are truly good for us and that guide our morality between wrong and right. The seed that will grow and will be rooted in knowing that evil is truly defined, not by who does it or says it but by a truly good and righteousness judge. That can direct the narrative that mankind seems to defy or deny and to say that human laws is their conscious, is truly contradictory of the simple, we can never seem to get it right. Perfection is an unreachable goal that is sometimes defined by numbers, such as a 100% on a test or a new record made by an athlete, who pushed the boundaries just that much farther. It is mind-bottling to say the least! What are your thoughts on it?

_____

_____

_____

_____

_____

_____

I'm not trying to be commercial and sale you a product, but to cultivate your thoughts to see through the copy and paste brainwashing on how life is through the media. It is hard to see a different angle from one camera lens. The dialogue and narratives of being different than others, who think the same thing, doesn't make anyone unique or different because everybody wants to be like everybody. When you choose to be someone other than yourself, that choice, destroys who you truly are in those few moments. The peer pressure of what is and who is liked or popular in a few moments of time comes to vanity. Death is an idea to the young and a due date to the old. The precious ticks seem to express the urgency to live the life you always wanted but is quickly ignored by the same clock that tells you it's time for work. How is it that we seem to be inspired by others from our youth, but we tend to forget inspiration isn't without adversity or patience to endure. Honestly, when it all boils down to it, you must see that inspiration, dedication, and motivation is a spiritual discipline that needs to be watered and nurtured to grow. I never saw a tree complain about the storm, but it only focused on growing to its fullest potential to face the storms to come. Just imagine how much time, effort, and resources it takes to grow that monstrous! Human nature tends to put limits, pretty much on everything based on history, personal experience, numbers, and forgetting that history had to be made, therefore, there had to be a first to push the boundaries and set the new possible from the thoughts or opinions of the impossible. We value words of others so much and some people even strive to live up to the opinions or criticism of others but, in the end of life not one single word will be placed in the ground with you. Doubt and expectation aren't worth the weight it carries on the mind and spirit. You shouldn't allow the opinion of others to dictate and influence your goals and dreams. People will hold you to your last performance, but at least you had the courage to perform whether it was a good or bad performance. Celebrate your failures with words of encouragement from the Lord and be happy about where you are in your life. The *American Dream* was built to enslave creativity and change what it truly means to succeed. The definition of success should be your God given dream, which utilizes your unique talents and skills given to you, to help others move into God's will in my opinion. The American Dream takes what was given to you and replaces it with success of monetary gain and fame that gives you a plastic purpose. By being put on a pedestal and being known, gives you plastic purpose and a role in the world. How subtle this message is spreading to the youth to show them that "making it" is to be on TV or do something great; that mankind can applaud or recognize. As a form of appreciation for your talents or skills, is to receive fame and money. People's opinions change and move like the ocean waves carried by a storm. Always changing with the "storm of opinions "and the craziest thing is that people value what others say since certain opinions feed your ego. A stadium full of applause seem to be a euphoric feeling for a narcissist. Nobody seems to sympathize or have empathy for others anymore. Let's be honest, our media over-saturates our minds with sex and violence in our video games, movies, and in our music of today. There is so much more to life than the behind of a stripper or the bling of a chain. That's too much stank for one day and maybe not everyone envisions having a big chain as" making it ". Whether we choose to admit it or not, we all are looking for what we love or enjoy. It feeds us in a positive way, which comfort us and helps us learn more about where we are in life. To make a self-note; life can get rough, but it also has its soft and most embracing moments as well. Time has also been an indicator, that forever on Earth is just a fairytale: told to give way to hope and security in an ever-changing world. It's hard to savor every moment, but we try to with videos and photos from that happiness frozen in time by the camera. The picture doesn't bring back the smells, tastes, laughs, or conversations that was had at that very moment. Who knew that your best friend in that time would become a distant stranger as time took its course, or your favorite place to eat has been closed down for good. Time brings a change to all things and all people, whether we wanted to accept it or not. I think the hardest part for me is that with growth, it's hard to relate to what you grew from. The roots are connected to the branches by the trunk of the tree, but they function in worlds apart and a similarity doesn't necessarily mean connection. The relation can be similarities that we all share to a point. A cocoa tree and a banana tree grow in the soil, but how they grow and how fast or slow, depends on the environment they are planted in. You are in a desert of doubt and confusion with a bottle of water of hope. When the environment supports thirst, you will be thirsty. So, plan on the environment that you want to be in. If I choose to grow in a negative environment, then I will produce negative fruit. But if I choose to grow in a positive environment, then I will produce positive fruit. How sweet is a banana to the taste buds. There is nothing like a sweet and healthy snack to get you going. The world doesn't believe that courage and discipline is essential to grow as human beings.

Courage is a trunk to stand tall in the face of adversity and discipline is the roots to focus on that development, regardless of the distractions, actions and decisions of others. We must decide what's the best resources for our trees to grow the strongest and endure the longest. Ask yourself where do your roots lie, in good soil or bad soil. So that you can evaluate, reconstruct, reflect, and analyze what is working and what isn't. My roots are firmly rooted in the bible that Jesus and his apostles preached. Peter to Paul, I learned something from them all; that my mistakes don't take away my growth, but my decision to stop growing does. People must see that self-love has disciplines; that you must obey, receive, and adjust to continue growing in an upward direction and not just in any direction. Who wants to grow a crooked tree with crooked roots and branches, not to mention crooked fruit. Talk about a taste-bud tongue twister and I don't think you would enjoy crooked or twisted fruit either. It's better to take the time with yourself to see where you are lacking;

so that you can pour water, sun, and a whole lot of patience into seeing it through until the end. I practice what I preach when it comes to sharing my core values with you. My pain and struggles are the reason why I smile and the reason my core values come to exist. What are your core values and are they helping your growth or are they depriving you from reaching your full potential?

_____

_____

_____

_____

_____

Awesome! I love the honesty and the realness of your answer. I like that we can relate on these topics, and this conversation has been nothing short of amazing. Sharing our thoughts with each other allows anxiety and loneliness to leave the room. A conversation that embodies community, unity, and connection like a bridge to a city or town. Some fear to connect with others because of the rejection, persecution, or criticism they may receive. Some fear to connect with God because of their own trauma and heart pains because of the comfort they already know from being emotionally and mentally guarded. The castle they have built is predictable in its design because with heart pains you will need to compartmentalize each situation into its' own room. It's locked away where no one can see, not even the bearer of the key because to recognize your pain would mean to recognize your flaws and weaknesses. Nobody wants to feel weak or hurt because our society today doesn't care to embrace you if you do have those weaknesses. I explore my flaws and weaknesses with Jesus Christ to get a better understanding of who I am and who I need to become. I don't want to be like any celebrity or influential person in the world, but I do desire deeply to be like Jesus Christ that existed over 2000 years ago. He lived a life without strife, sin and, malice with others in his 33 years of life. When you sit down and examine who he was, it will humble you away from the" good person "narrative that the world has put in place by those celebrities or influential people of our time. I copy what he has done in his life into my own, that allows me to examine my discipleship when I read my bible and not to be prideful of where I am in my relationship with God. This world will try to numb your spiritual senses by simulating your physical senses with drugs, sex, violence, and excitement. Some choose those distractions to distract them from their suffering and shortcomings in life and some choose to see the truth. Arrogance is bliss, right? No! arrogance is a choice to value your opinion above fact or truth. To believe in your "truth "is just your own lie that you like to be told. The world doesn't just deny the truth, but they also don't support the truth unless it's required to gain financial success or influence a propaganda in society today. Smoke and mirrors are the new movement that can give a title, but not the substance of the topic or subject. You need an example to refer to? *BlackLivesMatter* supported with its title the African American Community and their views on police brutality. But in its substance was to allow a message from the LBTGQ+ to be heard on a broader stage. A trojan horse, if you will, to validate their truths and ideas in subtle arrogance dressed in sophistication and adored in jewels of polished sympathy. That's why being weak isn't valued because it allows other sources,usually to hurt us more, to be our new distraction from our old pain. Therefore, I noticed when I searched the word for hope, joy, happiness; it doesn't hurt me more to receive it, but by reading I renew my spirit to begin a new day with courage, zeal, and passion that is far beyond my intellect. I enjoy the sunrise just as much as a sunset when it comes. Allowing my patience to be my strongest virtue and letting go of the passion for *"NOW"* and being more in love with *"IT WILL COME"* mindset, allows the spirit to be full of rest and refreshed. I never gained that from; caffeine, music, sports, people, traveling nor food. Those are all things that can refresh our minds and bodies, but not the human spirit that longs for a source that allows strength in our weakness to embody us greatly. To be grateful to just smile when it rains or to laugh in sad times, are things I once took for granted, but now I appreciate the small things so much greater than I did in my past. Evolution can't explain the longing to be loved and the ability to continue to love. Only God can, in my opinion, make all that was old and weary into something new and fresh. The smell of the new, excites the senses in certain forms such as the new car smell or the fresh look on new shoes. When you are new in an environment of the old, you will indirectly stand out from the rest. This isn't to put anyone on a pedestal because they have something new, but to imply that the mind can build habits that make you feel old or drained. The importance of healthy spiritual habits is vital to who you are and who you will become. Those habits can strengthen your mind, body, and spirit if you are willing to stay disciplined and evaluate your habits. You have to evaluate the source and the nature of your habits to hold yourself accountable. Accountability always accompanies responsibility, as it's confidant so you can express those inner habits into your actions that is received by others as good or bad. Not to contradict my other statement, but to advocate for the law that is set in place to protect you and me. Not every law is just or truly righteous, because most laws are written to protect or collect on someone actions. I had court on the 15th of February and I saw this man walking in chains for a crime he committed. As the proceedings went on I learned that the man was in chains because he had called his son for his birthday, but wasn't allowed to because of a court order that was in place. From my perspective, the man looked like he made an emotional decision towards someone that was important to him. Seeing tears in his eyes, he was remorseful for his passionate act that the law considered a crime. How could I say he was guilty or innocent? I couldn't, but I could relate to what he felt which was pain and sadness. My humility is what makes me a human being, a son, a father, a husband, and most of all a Christian. However, my humility does not advocate with lawlessness or having a reason to break the law when the law is there to protect you and your family. Therefore, I value the law on a personal level because I can evaluate my conscious on what is wrong and what is right; from what is the foundation that I can build on and not from my personal perspective or opinion, but what is ethical and morally good for all and not just for one or the other. Do the painter paints for his/her own satisfaction or to satisfy the perspective of the viewer? Mr. Da Vinci painted the Mona Lisa in 1503 and wasn't seen by others until 1516 or 1519. In that time, I wonder who or what inspired Da Vinci to paint such a capturing image. Inspiration can make a person's work immortal; as you can see, I can reference to an artist and his work from over 500 years ago. What is more valuable to you; to know your gifts and use them for yourself, or for the world to benefit from those hidden talents or skills?

_____

_____

_____

_____

_____

The value of talent makes us think of money or fame, but what about inspiration untapped by your talents not being known to others. The underground reservoir of inspiration sealed away by miles of "ground". The ground that is made up of doubt, selfishness, and negative thinking. Inspiration that inspires others to want to become inspiration is a powerful cycle because it's selflessness that plants the seed for it all. I guess to acknowledge that you have certain talents or skills can give a sense of self-identity. The world seems to acknowledge talent by the number of zeros on a check. Every talent must be paid for in the transaction of money for individuality seems to be the trend of the 21st century. I work hard to inspire, but I work even harder to stay inspired and to create inspiration. Inspiration has a big appetite for more inspiration to create more inspiration. I can look at the smallest of detail and receive some form of inspiration to add to my imagination. To imagine something that hasn't been seen or heard, is true belief that what you imagine one day will be. The one thought that transforms the reality of the next person is mind-blowing to meditate on. Everything we learn or use today, was a thought of some brilliant mind created by God to give us hope, a future, and a direction. Maybe it's just me or do you not think about things that were before you. How people lived and how they receive information to make decisions, whether good or bad. Our minds are our greatest tools to invent, inform, change, adapt, and react to any independent variable that may come. Life is really like the weather to me, because the weather doesn't dress for you, but you dress for the weather. Every lesson that comes in life, we must dress up for those circumstances. If we don't then eventually the lack of the proper dress will lead to more struggles and more pain. To dress up the mind for today's storm or rain, so to speak, can either be beneficial or destructive to you in the long run. Endurance is a part of life that seem to only be valued in sports and not in life in general. You must keep up with your mental conditioning to stay in shape and keep that inner focus to always have fortitude to reach and create new goals to progress forward in life. If your season is barren and cold, then your mindset should be of warm thoughts to keep your mindsight I call it from becoming frostbitten. If your season of life is summer, then your thoughts should always be hydrating to keep you from mental heat exhaustion. That's just a little wordplay to get you imagining what season you are in currently or what season is about to end in your life. Do you feel that your thoughts are healthy and growing, or destructive and wanting? Please share your thought with me.

_____

_____

_____

_____

_____

I see what you mean from what you have written. I imagine your answers to be from your perspective and truly relatable that I can take something from it. A dreamer will always dream and I, my friend, have a very enthusiastic imagination. It can get bubbly up there between my ears, but I try to let my bubbles get big with too many inventions and scenarios that seem to make me ponder, laugh and giggle inside. I never imagined that I would be writing a book until I did! I am now on my second book now which you are now currently reading at this very moment in time. I didn't let my mind be imprisoned by my thoughts, but I planted my thoughts in what I like to call mind-soil. Picture a rainforest of healthy and God-given thoughts being nurtured by the shine of hope and watered by the words of the bible. To say that my mind is imprisoned by my mind, is to say that my thoughts are criminal at its source; so, I organize my thoughts in a wild growth formation where every thought is helped by the next thought. I called it a mind ecosystem, where all my thoughts are independently dependent of each other indirectly, and sometimes directly helping the other to grow, to change, to stay consistent or constant. God's Holy Spirit help me build my

"Imaginary Amazon Forest "and like Adam helps me maintain the new growth. Time seems to either reveal or expose who we really are in the end. The product that is produced from our minds is truly our testament to who we say we are and what our actions show who we are. Not just magnifying lens or telescope that closes the distance to the object of interest at the time, but it's a process of baking a cake. You have different ingredients coming together to make a new purpose or a "cake ". How it tastes and looks dictates to you, the value of the cake itself. But not only the value of the cake is judged, but also the baker who chooses those ingredients to make it. The substance of the cake was important because the value and reputation of the baker was consistent with its previous tests from clients. The client, in this matter, is the people you meet and how you treat those people. People may not remember who you are or what you did, but they will remember how you made them feel. Some care about their character and other's not quite so much, based on their mindset and thought patterns they choose to embrace or change whether for the good or bad. Many ideas and innovative ways to think are on display because of technology. You may not be hungry, but the moment a commercial about fast food or restaurant pops up on the screen, your mind is receiving the information to your subconscious while you are in beta mode. The influence is so strong, that when you think about food within the next few hours from the time you watched the commercial, you will think of that fast food burger or that elegant restaurant to visit. The irony of not wanting to cook, but to get in your vehicle to travel to a place for someone else to cook something for you that is a complete stranger. Maybe it's just me, but I think about the psychology behind the marketing of food.

It's called color psychology in which you will look at a certain color and your mind will receive the information to compare what is more appealing to the senses or in other words your stomach. I'm only 27 years old, but my thinking process is of a veteran detective that is searching for the answers behind the traditions that I have known all my life. Ha! I guess you didn't see fast food as a traditional idea. tradition. It is because we are visional learners when it comes to fitting in with others. What to eat, what to wear, and how to style your hair seems to be the copy and paste of the mind. Maybe I enjoy organic food more than food mixed with synthetic materials." You are what you eat" is the slogan and I guess that means there are a lot of synthetic people in the world or maybe not; but let us continue with this conversation. Color psychology is using colors to engage and direct people to act. For example, yellow is for optimism, red is for energy or passion and white is for cleanliness, from my studies on color psychology. Have you notice that McDonald's have those exact colors used in their logo? You want a another one? Burger King uses red, yellow, blue and orange in their logo. They are saying to the public that they are trustworthy, determined, intellectual and creative subliminally. I will take a few moments to listen to a person when they discuss their favorite color. From there I can predict whether a person would rather have a banana or apple. If their favorite is yellow, then I can make a strong prediction that the banana will be the fruit of choice and vice versa with the red. My prediction may not be 100 percent accurate, but I will have better understanding of what appeals to a person more than not. I know not to put green apples or oranges in front of a person. The process of elimination and the limited choices a person can have, given me a stronger and more accurate hypothesis than before the conversation between me and another human being. Take a. The few moments to spend a little time by yourself and filter out the information you received today. Write your thoughts here. I want to know more about your day. You will realize that the information was being downloaded to your subconscious and will have influence on how you spend your time and your money. Any thoughts?

_____

_____

_____

_____

_____

_____

You will realize that the information was being downloaded to your subconscious and it will have influence on how you spend your time and your money. To control your subconscious is to be aware of your conscious, when you notice that beta mode is either a tool to help you or a tool for other's to steer you. The choice is yours when it comes to what information you will download throughout the day. Take a few moments to remember that every mind is special and unique, designed by a truly divine being by the name of Jesus Christ the Messiah. So, I choose to inform myself on the things that are in the fine details of the seams that are stitch together with precision, but we all know that human nature will never be perfect. Any last thoughts?

_____

_____

_____

_____

_____

Good talk, now let's go to Chapter Two …together !\

— CHAPTER 2 —
FEW MOMENTS OF TRUE EMOTION

To be passionate about something or someone is surreal, isn't it? The sensation or the thrill of being engaged in that very moment that embraces you. Passion seems to be the word used to describe someone's strong belief in something or someone greater than themselves. Most women are passionate about their makeup or hair when they are about to go out with friends and family, for brunch or to post on social media platforms, such as Instagram or Facebook to ultimately get likes and attention from others. Passion electrifies a crowd in an arena who are cheering for their favorite team that is winning or has won a championship. The expression of a person spirit towards something or someone is a passion that inspires the mind! To pursue with such zeal, can connect others to your journey in which will bring things you and that other person can relate on. Engaging with your emotions can seem like an ocean without a shore with no real place to sit and enjoy the view of it all. Our feelings illustrate to us who we are in our times of adversity and our times of great happiness. As a kid I was passionate about the outdoors because of how everything had its place, but still so wild and free. The birds flying high and the smell of barbeque in the air made me smile in awe. The smallest detail seems to interest me from a small ant hill to the elephant at the zoo. How big we feel in our own eyes until you've seen something that is bigger than your feelings, ha-ha irony huh? or is it just me with all my transparency? When you understand that passion is a healthy part of our journey, but it tends to hurt us if we overindulge in passion. See it's healthy to be passionate because that helps us act upon what we deeply love such as family, art, music, or a favorite sport. People feed off those people who live passionately or with an attitude of passion for life. Like I said before, it can get tricky when you allow your emotions to derail your train of common sense when it comes to certain situations in your life. Nowadays our culture supports toxic relationships or love because nobody wants to commit beyond what they are comfortable with and who they are comfortable with. It seems unappealing to go back to the same person that hurt me emotionally in my opinion, but some will choose to go through those cycles because of the thrill they receive from being hurt from the person they loved. I had a tattoo that said Love Brings Pain or L.B.P to say to whoever sees me that to love me truly will cause you pain. Real love will always require commitment to love even when there is no passion to love. Basically, what I'm saying is that if you go into a situation with a hidden motive to satisfy your need or wants from the beginning, it is only infatuation mixed with passion. You will boyfriend or girlfriend your emotions to death because of your lack to commit beyond how you feel. Sex and passion should not be the core of your relationship with someone who you truly want a long and healthy relationship with. In my opinion, the secret in marriage is God, patience, and sacrifice. Passion can have you wanting to pursue distractions for your selfish feelings to feed that monster with a unquenching and unsatisfying appetite. Nothing imaginary like the Loch Ness Monster or something, but a real enemy when left unchecked and evaluated can grow into something you don't even recognize anymore. It seems strange to be a stranger to your emotions and not long for that personal relationship with them. People's mission in life changes from loving deeply to not feeling nothing deeply as time goes on. What changed them, what do you think ?What situation changed you?

_____

_____

_____

_____

People's mission in life changes from loving deeply, to not feeling nothing deeply as time goes on. What change do you think?

_____

_____

_____

Drug use seem to be a truly fool's errand because it is dressed up as a cure for emotional pain and trauma. Wrapped in a bow with care and optimism from the vibrant colors of joy it seems to offer from the testimonies of those hypnotized by it. Our culture supports it and our music advocates for it with visuals from your favorite artist or celebrity. Usually giving the public eye, the O.K. or thumbs up to doing what makes you happy. Passion is a necessity for our emotional drive-in life. You can press the gas while in park and believe that the car will move, but in all reality that car will sit right there. True arrogance is arrogance when you choose to stay in stupidity for the simple fact or another. Our being is built on senses and nerves to give us awareness of what is going on. Pain will always be the best indicator that something is wrong and the drive to make things right. Passion can scrap your emotional drive because of the lack of maturity to understand each emotion with its own identity. The person that is your worst enemy, is you staring back through the mirror. Emotions expose your inner self to yourself and to others because they were meant to be the canvas in which you choose how to paint your life. You can paint angry or joyfully, however the canvas will only tell you who you are in the end. Not to look at our lives as a masterpiece to be put on a pedestal for everyone to see, but to examine your work with honesty and humility. A lot of people paint their lives by their sexuality or their sexual identity with extreme emotion, but with that identity the canvas will be painted on your core values, not anything else that people seem to say that would endorse your identity such as expensive brands or cars. Some people paint their lives in the public eye, which clarifies that having fame is part of their core values and that will be a part of their life canvas. Our thoughts are the paintbrushes, and our actions are the paint strokes.

What are you painting on your canvas?

A. Love

B. Anger

C. Sexual Identity

D. Fame

E. Money

My questions seem to be interrogative in nature, but really, I care about you as a person. Even though you are a stranger, which doesn't mean that we can't relate because we are completely human. The reason I believe God spoke in parables as Jesus of Nazareth is because he was trying to get the people to think spiritually about who they are, and that act alone, inspired me to imitate his character by asking the hard questions to speak to those hard feelings, that are layered like concrete over years of pain and hurt. I believe that everything I write is guided by the Holy Spirit and not by me in essence. The world advertises everything that is supposedly good for us. Why do you need to advertise something to someone to get them to believe something is good? If you believe it is good for you will try to see if it is or not. The subject of the matter is we want what is good, but it isn't here on Earth. The problem is we will lie to ourselves to make that lie seem like truth. People so used to people lying to them that maybe being lied to isn't so bad if whoever is telling it believes it to be true as well. We believe the person that is telling us the lie is truthful because most of the time the lies will come from someone you love. Real love doesn't play on your passion but funnels it away from pride and arrogance to show your true intentions on why and how you love. If the world accepts who you are because of a talent or gift, does the world really love you? Passion is beneficial when it is beneficial to others, that's why you must be careful with what and who you are passionate about. How deep a cut it is when, what, or who you are passion about doesn't show or produce that same zeal or energy that you put in. Now telling someone the truth even though it hurts them isn't called love, but verbal abuse in today's world. There isn't reproof or rebuke in letting a person who may be arrogant in their ways or a true narcissist that their actions does not match their words. The passion in saying *"I love you "* to someone that won't be in your life forever is the biggest lie that someone can use. Don't let your passion of infatuation destroy the passion to love and be loved. When I watched the movie *Collateral Damage,* I was moved by how relatable the movie was to my pain. How the actors felt what I felt even though the situation that caused the main actor's pain was different. The three things he was passionate about was time, death, and love in which he instilled it into his company. The main character name is Howard, who was at first a bright businessman with everything working for him. But as the movie proceeds his brightness fades away and the three ideals or pillars that he once believed deeply in were now what he hated. The death of his daughter broke his mind in two because he was fighting what he felt and what he knew. See it is easy to preach inspiration when you are winning or achieving your goals, but when something so strong comes and knock you on your knees, it changes your point of view. The mountain of comfort leveled to a valley of uncertainty by the immense emotional damage from loving someone or something shows your humanity and your fragility. Howard shows anger and denial throughout the movie until he meets the three platitudes that he once believed in. His friends compensated actors to be Time, Death, and Love to rejuvenate his mind. They wanted to get him back to the place of living life with passion! Death was an elderly Caucasian woman; Love was a young Caucasian woman and Time was an arrogant young African American man. All gave their responses to the letters that Howard had sent to them. They responded to his argumentative and emotional poetry to give him a new perspective on his pain. The pain was eating him alive, and he was falling apart wandering why. Through every experience he becomes more aware of his hurt and his emotions. Every situation filters out by the conversations he has with these three people as the movie grips at your heart strings. He gets to a point where he reconciles with his wife, by having those hard conversations and moments with his friends who care so much for him that when he sees that his lack of passion to heal and move forward with life was causing death to his company, his health, and the lives of employees. Which shows the domino effect of how our emotions or lack of it will corrupt us to hate everything about life. Life must be lived in a way that accepts the pain, the loss, and the loneliness of those situations that require us to go through life. A closed casket of a love one isn't an excuse to live a closed life, when love and passion requires an open heart to allow others to help and to be helped in their time and your time of emotional need. The worst prison on the planet is the life view on thinking that life is a prison and believing that it always will be. The rippling of one's emotions and thoughts from a rock consisting of doubt, fear, and hurt splashing into your pond of cognitive thinking. We tend to want to escape our thoughts, feelings, and our lives because of these events that are taking place that we had little control over. The outcomes seem to shape our hearts in ways we thought we could control, maybe even destroy. How hard is it to be comfortable in a space with no ceiling, no floors, and no walls of any kind? A place with no sound or light, but complete emptiness that some assume is the place to be. Yet, we notice home by the smells, sounds, and the visual beauty by heart. Home is the people we smile, laugh, and cry with as we go through life. Home doesn't seem like home when that person who made our heart's smile isn't there anymore. How we feel to fill that empty space with what we miss most; as you look and seek for smells, sounds, and visuals that

bring familiarity to your soul. The soul remembers those laughs and smiles of who or what is missed that was a catalyst for your happiness. Kind of selfish, in a sense, to deny time and space of who you love, as if your entitlement was a warning label to the universe or to God that your happiness could not be touched or changed by any means. Passion seem to be the fuel that accelerates our actions without the thought of reason. A foe that seduces common sense into a bed of intimate nonsense that seems to appeal to senses or the most empathetic sentiment that emancipate our feelings from the dullness and gray clouds of yesterday. As sand and heat make glass, so are our emotions and pain to heat into a clear picture of what is missing or maybe what should be missed to help you live and pursue far greater. Whatever greater that is for you in your own life is completely up to you. To know greater by pursuing greater takes a toll on the mind to want completeness. To be 80% healthy isn't the crime that convicts you but seeing 81% as the greater and not pursuing it, is the crime! is. Who knows what that 1% holds in detail, but it is best to be confidential about all the work you put in to get that 1%! Humility is the trait that we only like to use on certain occasions such as childbirth, weddings, and funerals. However, in day to day some tend to remove that image to reveal their selfish ambition. By the imagination you will get images of who that person is based on who they think they are and what they are passionate about. The care and energy invested into that passion can illustrate to you the life people see worth living. Most people's idea(s) of a perfect life is wealth, fame, and status of "importance "in society. Some may want to use their talents to change the world for the better or leave their mark on the world. As if though the world is capable of feelings and emotions. The people you want to notice you may have the same passion of wanting to be noticed. Passion is relatable because we can all share experiences of it, but it can be a crutch to who we are if we can't see that passion shouldn't be the source of our actions as much as we allow it to be. I would like to hear your last thoughts on this chapter.

_____

_____

_____

_____

_____

— CHAPTER 3 —
DEEP CONVO

As I sit in my thoughts, I appreciate the fight in my soul to desire positivity and light. Being a deep thinker about life and what my Creator wants me to learn and understand, seem infinite in possibility. I laugh to myself sometimes seeing how good life can be in our eyes based on what we can earn or gain. I learn to appreciate the journey of life like a hike. You will get the experience of the terrain on high hills and low trails underneath your feet. You will notice animals of all sizes and characteristics that come along the wood line. They all are different but bring an essential essence to your life. We seem to forget what we have experienced and tend to focus on the present moment. A lot times it is negative or troublesome to a lot of us but what God has showed me is that the greatness part of the hike is when the hike goes up hill. You feel the rocks underneath your boots and the little burn in your legs as you focus on getting to the top. Those birds you get to hear in the background of your hike show you that the best part of the journey is always fitted with challenges and obstacles. Those obstacles bring more value to the sight-seeing of the animals and the ecosystem they inhabit. You see the sunshine through the trees, that shines a little bit brighter or the flowers seem to be a little more colorful and vibrant. The details of life seem to be forgotten because of our pain and grieve. We decide that the hike is not worthy of experiencing no more because of the pain. We focus on generality of the hike instead of the spirituality of the hike. It seems to impose on our willingness to move forward and continue to enjoy the life that is around us. That flows through us and around us, however we let things clog our perspective on what we see and sometimes, let's be honest we choose to see what we want to see like life is just a channel that we can flip through.

We are always looking for the best show and whatever holds our attention for more than 8 seconds. Where has the contentment gone? Who are we without patience and humility? I may be rhetorically speaking to myself but I want to know your thoughts as well. Please share.

I never seen a tree complain about growing, have you? So why should we, when the storms in life are what makes us better human beings. Never forget the precious few moments that we have! Make the most of your life and don't waste it on vanity. Continue to hike my friends and never forget to enjoy every step of the journey.

Death, failure, and tragedy, seem to be the last things you would consider as a vital moment of life. We all have experienced these events regardless of age or gender. Some allow those events to control or imprison them, while others allow those traumatic events to change them, fuel them, and to inspire hope in the mist of the storm. There are moments in your life where you will look around for help or sympathy in people, but you won't find it. I experienced that feeling of complete shock and confusion of who those people really were to me. I felt what Jesus felt when he died on the cross. It wasn't that moment he died that convicted me most, but when he cried out to God the Father in heaven," My God why has thou forsaken me!" For the first time in a long time, my tears became my mirrors as they crystalize in my hands. It allowed me to see that Jesus protected someone who didn't love him back. That someone was me in all my limits and imperfections, so my eyes were opened to who love was. "THUD!" rang out as a bat hit my sheen bone at full force causing adrenaline to stampede through my body. The person that stood in front of me and the person that stood behind me were really my enemies, but I chose to protect instead of harm, even though hatred and violence flooded my very being. No! I'm not claiming to be a hero with a cape, because truly I couldn't even save myself. I was a villain with a white coat and a black heart, if I had to be honest. People that said they loved me, but secretly hated me were who I called brother, father, family, and friend. F.R.I.E.N.D? E.N.D, I never realize the "end" in friend, maybe because I wanted so badly to be good at choosing the right people. They were chosen because they had been abused, betrayed, or hurt and by that familiarity, our bonds so I thought, were pure and genuine. And just because I chose that path, doesn't mean others will choose that path as well. I was an infatuation for the infatuated, but never the object of true love. Being connected to someone by relation doesn't help your heart's navigation but aids the trespasser by the past experiences to reach you when it's convenient for those people. The very person I respected, laughed at my calamity which in turn matured my thoughts. My thoughts were like seeds in a tornado until I prayed. "I cried alone, felt hurt alone, and healed alone without the ones who I thought loved me. But regardless of conflicts, they made a choice. So, God, I'm here making mine. Show me a better way, Amen." Little did I know, my prayer was heard when I noticed my thoughts became grounded and sound. I moved with determination and resiliency like no other man. I found peace in the conversations of my camouflaged enemies, and I understood those boundaries should never be crossed. I grew out of the past, branched into my present, and bloomed in my season. My soil was God's grace, but my rain was my pain. What is your point of view on these subjects?

_____

_____

_____

Do you question the intentions of those around you?

    A. Yes

    B. No

    C. Maybe

The camera doesn't show our flaws, because we try to create the" picture-perfect" moment for the world to see. Nothing is as beautiful as it seems, and nothing is as strong as it seems. Tragedy was the lesson I paid attention to when it came. Those few intimate life moments that cause heartbreak and stress, amplifies the ugly and weakness in everyone. I failed in life so many times and in so many ways, but I never lost my optimism to succeed one day. I had a mind built on self-will and determination. Failure was always a good friend to me, being that it always told me the truth, regardless of how I felt about the situation. Failure exposed my highs and my lows, but more importantly it showed me people's character as well. Failure is a true necessity for what fuels you to be tested. The reward of failing than succeeding in life is expressed in currency and trophies. Every time someone stands out among the crowd, people gravitate to wanting to see what makes that person special. The "special" is failure fueling the discipline to stay focused on the goals that a person set for themselves each day. The trophies weren't the reward, but the journey to be persistent in who you are is the reward that truly expresses the "special" in us all. God gives us gifts to open, but if we never open them how will we know what we have been gifted with. Failure is the ribbon that is tied neatly around what is already there.

What is failure to you and what have you learn from your failures?

_____

_____

_____

Have you failed in achieving some of your goals so far?

A. Yes

B. No

I found inspiration in all these situations that can seem like an inconvenience to the human heart. My failures help me understand my beautiful imperfections in my humanity, but I'm not a failure just because I experienced failure throughout life. I probe my mind to figure out whether I devalued my failures because of my pride, or did I value failure more because of the humility it brought when I experienced it. The chaos of wanting to validate yourself belief to be truth so it won't be an emotional lie being told to deceive yourself from your own arrogance. The dream that is the catalyst to your actions to reach that position where you can say your life has an increased value, seem to be a logic choice to take. Death seems to slow you down to a point where you will analyze life in its stitching. The tapestry of elegance that is perceived in our eyes about life without analyzing what it means to live. My mother passed and it seems as if though I was a sports car in idle or neutral on the highway. I was a pedal-to-the-metal minded individual with reaching my goals and future inspirations. However, that all changed after I lost the person, I was trying to constantly prove myself to. I wanted to, but my mind was in cruise control enjoying the ride of life and avoid potholes, heavy traffic, and distractions in life. I slowed down to allow my emotions to catch up to my current situation. Death refocused my priorities on who and what I valued in life. The heartache seems to bring me out of a coma of illusions. Thus, allowing me to focus my attention on God even though I was angry, hurt, bitter, and lonely. I desired renovation into a design in my mind and I knew that only the one they called Jesus could do it. Who was I even if I accomplished every dream of mine. It seems by the accomplishments and the habitual success; I could answer with those titles and those descriptions of my abilities being recognized. Every award after my mother death had little meaning to my life in its essence. Stone and metal to describe who I was seem blissful, but also a bitter touch with the roughness or coldness of an award or trophy in my hand. When tragedy strikes, some believe it to be a jab, but really, it's a liver punch with a right hook or cross to the body so to speak with any consolidation. I valued tragedy as the reward of my arrogance. I was thinking if I worked hard enough it would validate my existence from the very moment I was born. My motives seem elementary based on how simple and bright I planned my life without respecting the concept that time waits for no man. The naïve belief that I would be where I need to be by this date or this date. I didn't value my hours of life the right way and cost me something, which were those precious moments with family and friends. It is May 8th,2022 and on Mother's Day I saw who I really was when I decided to serve through my grief instead of allowing my emotions to serve me. I serve my Pastor and his family as well as many other families in the church. With every thank you for a dish of this and a dish of that, allow me to understand the substance of love. It wasn't in the food, but in my customer service I was able to provide for those who needed nourishment. The cold and stony emotions eroded away with waves of maturity cooling my volcanic bosom to a new island with coconuts and wildflowers. My anger and hurt became the home for the birds of the air needing rest by my willing service to sacrifice not for praise, but purpose that punch through the ceiling of my feelings. Jesus led me by the peaceful waters like he said he would, but I didn't want to disappoint him in the episodes of last year playing in my mind with aside of popcorn for my flesh to criticize and scold. That sustainment was introduced to my new and innovative way of thinking through the mind of the Holy One! I was teary eyed about not being able to see the only person that seem to matter to me at one point in time, but when reality came back into my vision, it was clear that I was blind in my selfish emotion of the past hinting at my bruises and scars in such silhouette fashion designed to detail every garment of what was and wasn't. I supported the design with a sense of urgency, however, alterations had to be made by another designer. Truth had to be seamed into the fabric of my heart to address the home that was now someone else's. A tombstone replaced the imagery of my senses to see the paintings were different and the furniture was different in all fashions it forced me to let go differently, to let go spiritually was the conclusion of my essay in a sense. I watched as my wife laid flowers at my mother's grave which took me to a place where I wanted to be for once and that place was peace with seeing that the beauty of the flowers meet the ugly truth of that headstone where I laid my pride down and broke it into a million pieces. I glanced at her name and understood your name becomes the property of a headstone for the world to see. The living wanting to hang on to something of a loved one, but no not I, because I disliked the fact the headstone couldn't hug me back. No need for caption or social media post to describe today because honestly, I just want to live it! The greatest moment in my life is when I truly embrace it with open arms even if that means my warm embrace will leave me sometimes with a cold response. The moments like sitting down and talking with my grandmother about life and struggles. Hearing her wisdom with my heart to understand the message she is trying to teach me. Her eyes full of love and determination like sweet honey from the bees to an intense gaze of golden lava melting away all the ignorance youth had to offer. To listen to her life lessons allowed God to communicate with me in my own life to take heed of certain people and situations that maybe similar. I never thought that the place I was meant to be in, was the home that I grew up in as a youth. Preparation is always a necessity for performance when it is time. Usually, you would study a certain subject throughout the week to prepare for a test or quiz on Friday. So, when I read my bible and pray to Jesus about my day, I am preparing for battle with principalities and spirits of evil. I abandoned what I thought was right and adopted every truth the bible had to tell. My oldest son took me back to my childhood within myself when traumatic moments seem to poke at your humanity. I felt like a superhero in being able to be a role model for a child that loves me for me. What better hero than being yourself. A hero who doesn't have to wear a mask to protect who I am truly, but to embark on a journey that seems so full of scenery and beauty. A child will take you on a tour on how great you are to them when they know you are trying your best every day to love them. Love has a responsibility to the one whom you say you love. The opportunity will be crucial to your emotional development just as much as theirs. I set a path in my sights, and I ask my son to follow without a doubt he said, "I'm ready dad!" with this look of bubbly admiration. In that moment I wanted to cherish his emotions and challenge his perspective. So, we started on this gravel road, side by side and hand in hand. Along the way he said," Dad I'm tired.", and unlike the world I acknowledged what he felt. So, I put him on my shoulders, and I continued to jog forward with a determined pace. I wanted to show him when you love someone deeply, you will carry that connection or bond when life seem to beat the other person down. He regains his energy like no other 5-year-old baby boy would do. As we approach the stop sign, I pushed him forward to reassure him that he was more important than me reaching my goals. As I raised my hands in celebration for his victory, I was amazed with his attitude to endure through the fatigue. The road that we jogged lead to my belated mother's grave site and I discovered like a archaeologist, that the discovery of what was underneath my pain was love, joy, and happiness wasn't what satisfied my being but the journey was in essence the true discovery. To be loved by someone who appreciates you is a blessing a lot of us think we deserve but no not I. I knew to be a father I was under-qualified and underserving of such a gift." DADA!" from my other baby boy seem to shock my nervous system with 10,000 volts of happiness. The hugs and kisses I give to him don't seem to be enough for time to pause for a while. To just enjoy how great, they were in my eyes. Fragile but strong enough to empower those who have been searching for love for a long time. The Lord God has blessed me in my frailty and my humility that gave me identity that separated me from my past, but also separated my future from my present. Those who are heart-broken in life is because the one who said they love you didn't understand the responsibility behind those words. Those who say those words don't want to pick up the responsibility of another for them to grow because sin will never look to be responsible for anything other than the bearer. Fatherhood gave me the answer to my broken childhood like fallen leaves in the autumn wind. I couldn't hold on to my branch like questions without the wind of a thousand other ones pulling me in my emotional weightlessness. The whys of yesterday became the truth of my today because through love, not just love but sacrificial love I learned the truth. The truth was that I had responsibility that no one wanted to take each every day with me as a kid. My kids are not my blood, but by our love, we are family. I wrote this book to help you examine yourselves, but again my Savior has allowed this book to examine me and where I am. The intimacy of his approach seems to teach me that love isn't just a feeling, but a sacrificial action that continues without a single thank you or applause. The love that says," You're welcome "no matter if it was appreciated or recognized. It seems unfair but just for a warrior who is willing to not let his or her battle scars dictate their character because within a scar of permanency is stitches of pain, beating with every heartbeat.

Any blessing that you are grateful for? If you are then it would be my honor to hear your thoughts.

    A. Yes
    B. No

_____

_____

_____

_____

The journey of this conversation is something that I would say is a gift that keeps on giving. I always been the one who liked to give a gift than to receive one. The fulfillment of the happiness you can give to someone by just being kind or empathetic is truly wholesome for those who partake in the moment. Some of the biggest moments of my life was listening to people stories of their pains and joys. Sharing my time to just understand another human being regardless of their status or race. A heart has no color, no territory, or team; but only an emotional connection sparked by the deep fires of those around us that seem to inspire our inner being like no other. The only difficulty is not to be difficult about your difficulties and shun others away from your life. Social media seem ideal for hypercriticism. Hear me out on this one will quick. The loners don't look to be known but look to be known through how they see themselves like a clear divider between test-takers at the end of the school year or semester. We long for privacy break in well what seem like an everyday routine to zoom in on what makes us happy, excited, joyous, or inspired. Never about what gives us relation between each other in this life. The narrative is always to save face for faces that seem to only care for entertainment from their everyday routine to maybe escape a cycle by biking up a mountain of excellency or to a valley of mediocrity. Strange to say what we desire isn't the defining moment of our lives, but just the image of it. There is no true substance to the art from the "artist" in; saying this I want to imply the very nature of personal connection cannot obtain the nature of the person in a 24-hour span or even 24-year span. What if social media was seen from the eyes of God. What would he post that may change your definition of what is extraordinary or who for that matter. I'm not trying to save face has if I don't use social media but I simply narrate as author should, what hasn't been seen or want to be seen. The filter or funnel seem so small that only one perspective seem to blow through with so many life experiences happening each second it does life no justice at all. I'm a little offended that what shines or what is popular is what should intrigue my brain cells for 8 seconds or so. Ha-ha,I guess the joke is on me, even though it maybe, my sense of humor keeps me bright like the lighthouse facing the storm bringing ideas that are in the open sea to come out of the waves of indecisiveness and confusion. Where do your thoughts take you?

_____

_____

_____

_____

— CHAPTER 4 —
THE NOMAD

My teenage years were nomadic to say the least and maybe I liked it that way to really understand who I was going to become. I didn't realize what a nomad was until my 9th grade Geography class, but I found it interesting the way a group of people accepted not being in a situation longer than the environment would support. So right there and then I accepted that ideal that I wasn't going to continue to embrace what my emotions didn't want to support. My loyalty wasn't nomadic, but static because it was an environment that supported my nomadic emotions at the time. I embrace a nonchalant and stoic view as I grew older as a teen not realizing how ice cold I was becoming through the season. My veins became like the very streams of winter and my tears became like the snow that I traveled in.

Living in an ice age of cold normality when relationships shattered like a frozen pond. Allowing others to feel what I grew numb to because I was trying my best to protect the little happiness I had left. Polar bears, Mammoths, and saber-tooth like characters seem to sniff me out to feed or keep me from my destination. My nomadic state helped me survive my freezing perspective to not get comfortable with the valleys or the cold. Only embracing the moment, it starts and the moment it ends. Letting goes of old skins form last winter and pursuing new prey for meat and clothing seem primitive, but this was my normalcy or if I'm politically correct my normality. My anger formed icebergs that could rip through any titanic of affection to reveal its inner workings. Which allowed me to understand that it wasn't a relationship worth sinking with. I AM TRULY A NOMAD IN THIS 21ST CENTURY. Thank you for coming along this personal and heartfelt journey with me. I never forget you nor what you have shared with me. This may be the end of this book but not the end for us, my friends!

Prologue

I looked pain in her eyes. She taught me something I never realize that she told only truth because she came from many lies. Her windows cut me with her broken glass. As my soul glazes into her past. Her silo displayed her disdain for heroes. No one came to save her. So, she always singing a song of great fantasy. Oh, pain how gentle your songs play. Music of peace and harmony

Brings hope. Brings direction. Brings love.